U Turn

5 Simple Steps To Achieve Success Starting Now

ZEESHAN RAZA

Published by Smart Ideas Publishing

Copyright © 2016 Zeeshan Raza

All rights reserved. No part of this book may be reproduced by any mechanical, photographic, or electronic process, or in the form of phonographic recording; nor may it be stored in a retrieval system, transmitted, or otherwise copied for public or private use without the prior written permission of the author, except by a reviewer who may quote passages in a review.

978-0-9937090-4-3

This material has been written and published for education purposes only. The reader understands that the author is not engaged in rendering medical advice or services. The author provides this information, and the reader accepts it, with the understanding that people act at their own risk and with full knowledge that they should consult with a medical professional for medical help.

The author shall have neither liability nor responsibility to any person, or entity with respect to any loss, damages, or injury caused, or alleged to be caused, directly or indirectly by the information contained in this book.

The intent of the author is only to offer information of a general nature to help you in your quest for achieving your goals. In the event you use any of the information in this book for yourself, which is your constitutional right, the author assumes no responsibility for your actions.

Do It Anyway

People are often unreasonable, irrational, and self-centered.
Forgive them anyway.

If you are kind, people may accuse you of selfish, ulterior motives.
Be kind anyway.

If you are successful, you will win some unfaithful friends and some genuine enemies.
Succeed anyway.

If you are honest and sincere people may deceive you.
Be honest and sincere anyway.

What you spend years creating, others could destroy overnight.
Create anyway.

If you find serenity and happiness, some may be jealous.
Be happy anyway.

The good you do today, will often be forgotten.
Do good anyway.

Give the best you have, and it will never be enough.
Give your best anyway.

In the final analysis, it is between you and God.
It was never between you and them anyway.

What is reproduced above was found written on the wall in Mother Teresa's home for children in Calcutta.

CONTENTS

	Introduction	1
Step 1	You've Got the power	12
	Our Connection with Others	
	Training Your Mind	
	Exercises to Train Your Mind	
Step 2	Unleashing the Genie	28
	The Clearing Process	
	Does the Idea of Setting Goals Bore You?	
	The Process of Goal Setting	
	Tracking Your Progress	
Step 3	Improving Your Self-Image	46
	What Is Self-Image	
	The Ego	
	How to Improve Your Self-Image	
Step 4	Creative Imagination	65
	What Is Creative Imagination or Visualization?	
	What Role Does Visualization Play	
	A Few Notes on Visualization Practice	

Creating Focus

Rating What You Want

Imagining a Scene

Feeling It

Let Go and Have Faith

What's Big? What's Small?

Clearing

Forgiveness

Step 5 Nailing it to the ground   94

Reinforcing a Goal

Generating a Positive Perspective

Conclusion   117

Inspiring Resources   120

Acknowledgements   124

About the Author   125

INTRODUCTION

"Khudi ko kar buland itna kay har taqdeer say pehlay Khuda banday say khud puchay, bata teri raza kya hai"

(Raise yourself to such heights that before creating your destiny, the Universe itself would ask you, "What is your opinion about this?")

~ Sir Allama Iqbal (1877–1938), Poet, philosopher, and great thinker

Back home in Pakistan, our elders used to say that young children shouldn't look in the mirror. As is the way with the younger generation, we never really paid any attention to such "old wives' tales." However, now that I think of it, this makes perfect sense. As soon as children see themselves in a mirror, they create an image of themselves. At that very moment, they start a life-long journey with a self-image, which, in most cases, restricts them from realizing their full potential. This is not to say that we should not ever look at ourselves in the mirror, but when we create an image of ourselves, and then define ourselves by that image, we prevent our own growth.

In this book, I present a process, which, once mastered, you will be able to shed any preconceived notions about yourself and take control of your life. Though some of methods may be familiar to you, it's how you use them that matters. My goal is to give you exercises and practices that you can use in your daily life to transform your current situation. I have already accomplished this, and so can you! The key is to hang in there and not give up.

Each chapter in this book is dedicated to one of five steps that you need to transform your life: (1) You've Got the power, (2) Unleashing the Genie, (3) Improving your self-image, (4) Creative Imagination, and (5) Nailing it to the ground.

1. You've Got the power

Emotional intelligence is a term coined by Daniel Goleman in his book *Emotional Intelligence: Why It Can Matter More Than IQ*. Put simply, emotional intelligence is the ability to use your emotions in an intelligent way. It's the ability to manage them, rather than letting them control you. Once you master the art of managing your emotions, it gives you immense power over others.

Many of the books that talk about visualization, affirmations, and similar concepts assume that the reader knows what emotions are. However, more often than not, we are taught in school, at university, from the media, and from our society to suppress our emotions. This is because these influences project only the physical aspects of our lives and consider success to be measured by accomplishments, such as getting a degree, a car, or a well-paying job. There is no mention of how these achievements could ultimately allow us to fulfill our emotional needs, such as happiness and being at peace with oneself. Therefore, the first step to changing your life is to create emotional intelligence so that you understand your emotions.

Emotions have the same role in your road to success as a GPS has when you are driving to a new destination. Though you know that the destination exists, you don't know what route to take.

"Your intellect may be confused, but your emotions will never lie to you."
~ Roger Ebert (1942–2013), America film critic, journalist, and screenwriter

Once you understand what your emotions are, you will understand the guiding system that can take you to the life you desire. This brings us to the next question: Do you even know what you *really* want in life?

2. Unleashing the Genie

Rather than keeping vague ideas in your mind about what you want in life, it works wonder when you write your ideas down as goals. Setting goals brings clarity to your mind as it shifts ideas that were in the background to the forefront. We have various thoughts about what we want in life, but the exercise of writing down your goals makes it easier for your conscious mind to focus on them. Just as when you are driving to a new destination, whether you use a map (like in the good ol' days) or a navigation device, you *have* to define the location you are driving to.

3. Improving Your Self-Image

Once you have written down your goals, you can begin to work toward achieving them. As often happens, while you were writing them down, you might have noticed that your mind was telling you that your goals are not achievable.

Have you ever wondered what's the difference between you and Warren Buffett? Or between you and Mother Teresa? We are all made of same flesh and blood. We all have a number of opportunities in life. What's different is what we think of ourselves and our limitations.

"When you change the way you look at things, the things you look at change."
~ Wayne Dyer, American self-help author and lecturer

Working on your self-image is an important step. As you progress, you will realize that it's your own thoughts that hold you back. One of the ways to improve your self-image and realize your goals is what is called *visualization*.

4. Creative Imagination

In creative imagination or visualization, you focus on one goal and imagine that it has already been realized; you feel what it would be like to have achieved that goal. It is a kind of daydreaming, except that it is accompanied by emotions and is highly effective for creating a sort of prototype of the real-life experience before it materializes.

"All prosperity begins in the mind and is dependent only upon the full use of our creative imagination."

~ Ruth Ross, American psychologist and author

5. Nailing it to the ground

The last step to transform your life is the use of *affirmations*, which are positive statements pertaining to your life or certain goals. Affirmations bring you one step closer to actualizing your dreams. They are not lies; they are true representations of your dreams. These statements pull your dreams from the world of thought to the realm of physical reality. In this section of the book, you will find affirmations on various topics. You will be able to modify them to suit your own situations.

The Question of How?

When you are writing goals, or even thinking about achieving big things in life, the question that will come to your mind is "how?" You may think, "I don't have enough education or money, and my health isn't good enough. How will I ever be able to achieve these goals?"

These thoughts alone can discourage you from going any further. However, take this simple example: Imagine you are standing in front of your refrigerator and would like to open the door. What do you do? Do you think about how to do it? Do you worry about whether or not your muscles will respond and help you open the door? Unless you, unfortunately, have a physical disability, you are able to open the refrigerator door, having full faith that you can do it.

Just as you may not be aware of the complexities of the way your body works to allow you to you to open that refrigerator door without thought, so the Universe has provided you with everything in abundance, and a continuous flow of prosperity can come your way. Only when you accept that it is possible, you can and will live the life that you dream about.

Many people make the mistake of trying to figure out how their goals can be achieved. However, just as you are able to walk and talk, you have the resources to realize your dreams. Just as you don't need to worry about how your tongue will move when you decide to talk, you do not need to think about how your goals will be achieved once you decide to achieve them.

This is not to say that you do not need to work for them. You need to take some kind of action. However, the Universe has abundant resources at its disposal, and once you have faith that your life will change, things will start happening in the most unexpected ways. That is my promise to you. People, resources, and circumstances will start to show up.

You do not need to tell the Universe how to give you health, or from where to give you that extra source of income. All you need to do is set your goals, visualize them as already realized, reinforce them with affirmations, and continue to have faith that things are about to change.

Throughout this book, I refer to the Universe. Most of us believe that there is one source from which all blessings and powers flow. Some call this power God, some call it Allah, and others call it the Creator, universal energy, and so on. For simplicity, I call it the Universe. You can replace it with whatever term resonates with you.

I wrote this book to share what I have learned, understood, practiced, and achieved. I want to help as many people as possible; however, if I can change one person's life for the better through my words or actions, I feel I will have realized the purpose of my life.

At the end of the book, I share a list of some inspiring movies and books, as well as some online resources that might help you create a positive outlook on life. They have inspired me in taking various so-called bold steps in life. I hope they will do the same for you.

May you be blessed with a life full of purpose and contentment. Amen.

STEP 1: YOU'VE GOT THE POWER

"We define emotional intelligence as the subset of social intelligence that involves the ability to monitor one's own and others' feelings and emotions, to discriminate among them and to use this information to guide one's thinking and actions."

~ Peter Salovey, Professor of Psychology, Yale University, and John D. Mayer, Professor of Psychology, University of New Hampshire

In his bestselling book *Emotional Intelligence: Why It Can Matter More Than IQ*, published in 1995, Daniel Goleman introduced the concept of emotional intelligence (EI). In this book, he successfully demonstrated that emotional intelligence is a stronger indicator of success than IQ. I believe this was the first time the idea of using IQ testing as a guide for determining success or failure in life was challenged. Goleman cited various cases to prove that people who had very high IQs had actually failed many times in the face of life's challenges. He made the point that it is people's ability to manage their emotions that leads them to success in life. Much research has taken place in the field of emotional intelligence. One of the more significant contributors to the field is the Consortium for Research on Emotional Intelligence in Organizations. Please see the section "Inspiring Resources" at the back of the book for their website, where you can find recommended books and research articles. Several tools have also been developed to assess an individual's EI. One such tool is the Mayer-Salovey-Caruso Emotional Intelligence Test (MSCEIT).[1]

Simply put, emotional intelligence is the ability to manage your emotions in any situation. This requires creating self-awareness. Awareness of how your emotions affect your thoughts and behavior. How do you react to various situations in your life? Do you respond immediately with uncontrolled

---

[1] John D. Mayer, Peter Salovey, David R. Caruso, and Gill Sitarenios, "Brief Report: Measuring Emotional Intelligence with the MSCEIT V2.0," *Emotion* 3, no. 1 (2003): 97–105, http://heblab.research.yale.edu/pub_pdf/pub55_Measuringemotionalintelligencewiththe MSCEITV2.0.pdf.

outbursts? Or stop to reflect before you react?

Let's take an example: You are sitting in your office and one of your assistants walks in and starts shouting at you. She has a problem with one of the customers and is blaming you because of a new process you recently introduced that she believes caused the problem. Now there are two ways you can react to this:

Option A: You think, "How dare she barge into my office and shout at me like this! How can she blame something on me when she herself doesn't understand the process?" You yell back at her with an even louder voice, and you both end up in an argument. She goes to your boss to complain, and it becomes a Human Resources issue.

Option B: You let her finish talking. You give her time to get it out of her system. Then you repeat the problem in your own words, removing the blame and other aggressive statements that she had used originally, and then you say, "Did I understand you correctly? Is that the problem as you see it, or should I restate my understanding?" She would then either agree or make modifications. Next, you need to figure out why she behaved as she did. What was bothering her? Often, people get frustrated when they are asked to step out of their routines and do something different. Most likely her frustration was rooted in having to deal with a new process, or perhaps she hadn't understood the process clearly in the first place. You can establish this by saying that you just want to confirm if you had explained the process properly. If she seems unsure of it, then you can explain it to her again. All along, you speak calmly. In almost all circumstances, this will resolve the issue right there and then.

Now my question to you is: What option would you have chosen if you were in this situation? If you do not have an assistant working under you, assume it's your boss who yelled at you.

Many people would choose option A. And *that* is why I decided to write this book. Usually, I say, that the difference between those who have made it in life (winners) and those who continue to struggle (not winners yet) is that those still struggling either do not recognize their faults, or, if they do, they never do anything about it, and winners, on the other hand, not only recognize what's holding them back, but they also take powerful actions to overcome their limitations.

If you have read this far in, you are already on your way to success!

The scenario above could be similar to any other kind of argument, such as between a husband and wife, a parent and son, and so on. In the office scenario discussed above, more important than asking how you would, or should, react is, how do you develop the attitude to react in a way that brings about a positive result?

Our Connection with Others

Scientists have been studying this world of ours for many years. In modern science, researchers have discovered that we are surrounded not only by energy, but our bodies, and even our thoughts, are made up of energy as well. This energy vibrates at different frequencies. You may be familiar with this concept from your own reading or from programs on TV and other media.

The German theoretical physicist and winner of the Nobel Prize in Physics in 1918, Max Planck (1858–1947), said, "As a man who has devoted his whole life to the most clear-headed science, to the study of matter, I can tell you as a result of my research about atoms this much: There is no matter as such. All matter originates and exists only by virtue of a force which brings the particle of an atom to vibration and holds this most minute solar system of the atom together. We must assume behind this force the existence of a conscious and intelligent mind. This mind is the matrix of all matter."

The core of everything we see and feel is energy, there are no separations, no boundaries. Everything around us is energy vibrating at different frequencies. There are no differences between you and me. You belong to the same energy that I do; however, in our modern society, we have developed the idea of *me*. *I* want this. *I* want that. How could he say that to *me*? But in reality, we are all one and the same and connected. So when people do something bad to us, they are hurting themselves as well. By the same principal, if we do something good for someone else, we also do it for ourselves.

The only difference is perception. You may have noticed that you are extra kind to people you love. You overlook their faults, don't complain about their mistakes, and so on. But if your relationship with someone takes a wrong turn, you don't overlook even the smalles of things.. The reason for this is that when all is going well in your relationship, you see the other person as an extension of yourself; he or she is a part of you. However, when things are disrupted, you disconnect from the other person and, therefore, develop a negative attitude toward the person.

In reality, however, you are not disconnected. Think of the power that runs through your apartments, offices, and houses to run devices such as computers, printers, TVs, game consoles, and appliances. Just as these are all powered by electricity, so are we all connected by energy.

What has gone wrong is that we have assumed that we have disconnected ourselves from the one source. There is a central energy that runs through everything. We need to stay aware of this mentally. . Our egos are just illusions. Self-awareness is the realization that we are all one and we are able to control our reactions.

Technique for Connecting with Others

Imagine that you are driving in slow traffic and you feel a sudden thud on the back of your car. You look around and the driver behind you is getting out of his car. You get out in a rage, thinking, "There is already a traffic jam, and this stupid driver didn't put his foot on the brake, and now I'll have to go through the hassle of getting my car repaired!" However, when you get out of the car, you see that the other driver is your best friend. He apologizes and says he will get your car fixed. You smile, telling him that it's okay; you'll take care of it.

How can one who was so angry and upset suddenly become so pleasant? That, my friend, is managing your emotions. We do it every day without even realizing it. All we need to do is to learn to do it more often. If you can master this, you are on your way to happiness in all circumstances.

Let's take another example. You get home from the

office and see an unpaid bill that was due yesterday still lying on the couch. You ask your spouse if she paid it, and she says no. She tries to say something, but before she can, you start yelling, saying you are so busy at work and have so much on your plate and why couldn't she have taken care of it. When you finish, she says, "Honey, you told me yesterday that you would take care of it." Now you remember, and you sheepishly apologise..

Again, observe the change in behavior. This is another example of managing your emotions and moving from anger to love and caring. We do this day in and day out.

Caution: Managing your emotions does not mean that you suppress your anger or anxiety. It means you feel connected with others. That's why you try to understand why others behave the way they do, even if you do not know them. When you do that, you can't feel the hate toward them because you now see them as extensions of yourself. Suppressing your feelings is very harmful and not suggested at any level.

Training Your Mind

In his book *Psycho-Cybernetics: A New Way to Get More Living*

Out of Life, Maxwell Maltz, discussed research done by Dr. Edward C. Tolman, a psychologist and expert on animal behavior at the University of California In this research Dr. Tolman concluded that humans as well as animals create what he called *brain maps* or *cognitive maps* when learning about their environment. These maps are broad and general when learning takes place and when there isn't a crisis. However, if learning takes place in a crisis situation, the map they create is limited.

He had conducted experiments on rats that were well fed and had sufficient water and were permitted to roam about and explore a maze. To a general observer, it seemed that the rats did not learn anything. However, if the same rats were placed in the same maze again while hungry, they showed they had learned a great deal by quickly and efficiently going to the goal. Other rats that had not had the opportunity to learn the maze and create maps and were put in the maze while hungry and thirsty became frustrated and had difficulty reaching the goal in the maze. These rats could find only one "correct" route to the goal. If this route were blocked the rats became frustrated and had great difficulty learning a new one

We have fire drills in our schools, offices, and apartments to teach us how to react when a real emergency occurs. As observed in Dr. Tolman's research above, our minds can discover better solutions to problems when those problems are not faced in an emergency.[2] When we have ample time to think and react. It is when we have time to plan that we can be successful in our decisions. When we know what we might expect and how to respond before a fire breaks out, we are training our minds.

Our minds are tools—very powerful tools. However, we have taken away the mind's power by becoming slaves to it, often influenced by our egos, rather than controlling it and using it as a tool. We use our minds to try to understand how our minds work, like a computer trying to understand the workings of another computer.

---

[2] Edward C. Tolman, "Cognitive Maps in Rats and Men," *Psychological Review* 55, no. 4 (1948):189–208.

"If you use your mind to study reality, you won't understand either your mind or reality. If you study reality without using your mind, you'll understand both."

~ Bodhidharma (fourth and fifth centuries CE), Buddhist monk

The fact is, we control our minds; we are not our minds. This is the key to understanding the difference between those who make it in this life and those who only dream about making it.

We all have a higher self—a self that sits above our bodies, including our minds. Let's call it our souls for the sake of this discussion. We lose control of our lives and get into trouble when we confuse our minds with our souls and follow the paths our minds lead us along.

Perhaps you have heard about this new breed of computers that think on their own. These computers are said to have artificial intelligence. Well, okay, but humans were behind their development, telling them what to think and what problems they needed to focus on. Letting our minds control our lives is similar to letting this new generation of intelligent computers think on their own without any human involvement.

So how do you differentiate between yourself and your mind? Let's revisit the scenarios we discussed earlier: the guy who changed his behavior from anger to love, and the man who became more compassionate when he realized it was his friend who had hit his car. When you manage your emotions and act with compassion, you are behaving as the real *you*. *You* can develop it into a habit—if you do it often.

In an interview, Daniel Goleman described a technique using emotional intelligence, whereby school children used red, yellow, and green traffic lights to help them stop and think before they responded so they would learn to manage their emotions.[3] You can use this same concept to develop emotional intelligence in your adult life. When you are faced with a situation where an emotional outburst is possible, imagine yourself standing in front of a traffic light. The first color, red, tells you to *do nothing*; this means do not react and say or do

---

[3] John O'Neil, "On Emotional Intelligence: A Conversation with Daniel Goleman," *Creating a Climate for Learning* 54, no. 1 (1996): 6–11.

what comes to your mind right away. The next color, amber or orange, represents the *evaluation* phase. In this phase, you analyze the situation and how best to react emotionally. This is where you try to understand why the other person reacted the way they did. The final stage, green, is for *go*. By this stage, you had not reacted to the stimuli, but stopped and thought about it, and now you know the best way to react and can take the action. This is an excellent tool to react appropriately, using your emotions in an intelligent way. Please see the Inspiring Resources section at the back of the book for a listing of Daniel Goleman's book *Emotional Intelligence* and an EQ toolbox website.

Exercise to Train Your Mind

I recommend that you do this exercise daily until you feel you are in control. You can then reduce its frequency to every weekend. Create a log of your interactions with others when you expressed your emotions. These could be anger, being upset or frustrated with someone, showing love and affection, being sad, or being cheerful and happy. The purpose of this exercise is to create awareness of your current situation. The log is not meant for you to be judgmental toward yourself, and you need not show it to anyone, so just be truthful. You can use the following log as an example.

Log of Emotional Responses

Date	16 March 2013
Situation	A friend didn't show up at my birthday party at the very last minute, citing some urgent matter she can't discuss right now.
Emotion	I got really angry and upset with her and told her not to call me again. I was disgruntled and hard to get along with during the party.
Was this reaction appropriate?	No

How could this have been better?	I know my friend must have a good reason. I will ask her tomorrow. This is my party, and I have waited for it so long, so I am going to enjoy it.

When you are logging these events, think of them as being in the past. Ask yourself how do you think you should have reacted? Keep in mind that we are all connected. Egos do not exist in reality, and what we send out to others does come back to us.

Please see the Inspiring Resources section at the back of the book for the "Skills Converged" website, where you can find free training materials for increasing your emotional intelligence. The field of emotional intelligence is vast, and we have just touched the surface. However, you can begin to recognize when you are faced with certain situations that might trigger outbursts of emotion, and then be able to manage your reactions rather than letting your emotions control you.

Step 2: Unleashing the Genie

"Setting goals is the first step in turning the invisible into the visible."

~ Tony Robbins, American self-help author and motivational speaker

You are reading this book for one of three reasons. Either you are not achieving anything that you want to achieve, you are achieving some but not all of your goals, or you are achieving much of what your want, but you want to improve. In any event, you have something you want to achieve.

Many people today want more money. I would like to emphasize that aiming for money is fine, but what do you want to do with it? This is the big question that many are unable to answer. The reason? They have never thought about it. Before reading the beautiful book by Shakti Gawain called *Creative Visualization*, I was the same. I wanted a ton of money, but had you asked me then what I would do with it, I would not have had a definite plan.

Setting goals might seem like a boring exercise if viewed as an activity on its own. But if you understand its far-reaching effects, it becomes very interesting. Let me tell you a real-life story about how goal-setting made one of my long-sought-after goals a reality. Interestingly, I had very little to do with the outcome.

I have a younger brother. His name is Karrar. For many years, I wanted him to come to Canada; however, since I had moved here, the government had removed the category of professionals under which Karrar would be eligible to apply for immigration. In short, there was no way he could come here. When I sat down to write my goals, one was to bring him to Canada. This is what followed:

Soon after writing down my goal, I learned that the government was opening up the immigration policy, and that Karrar would be eligible to apply for immigration. Then I read about the services of a well-known immigration lawyer on a LinkedIn forum. I wrote to him to say that I was interested in his services for my brother, and then we spoke. Surprisingly, he was about to visit his mother in the town in Pakistan where my brother happened to live, so I arranged for them to get in touch with each other. The lawyer's mother wasn't well, so he had to prolong his stay, which made it possible for my brother to enter into a contract with him. My brother's application is in process and we were about to see one another after more than three years.

All of this happened only after I had written down what I wanted. Somehow I had attracted the forces needed to help me reach my goal, and it happened within a few months. Are you interested in seeing your goals realized? This is how I did it:

I sat down with the decision that I would get up only when I had written my heart's desires on a piece of paper. There are two points to remember when you do this:

1. Write down whatever your heart desires, regardless of limitations or restrictions that you think exist. Write as if you were the creator of your life. Imagine that you are writing a story and creating a character. You can do anything with the life of this character. Would you feel any limitations if you were creating a character? Think as if everything were possible.

2. Goal-setting is not meant to restrict your ambitions in life. Once written, you can change them daily, weekly, or whenever you like. The key is to keep revisiting them and amending them as necessary.

"Imagine that you are writing a story and creating a character. You can do anything with the life of this character."

Caution! While writing your goals, you need to be specific; write exactly what you would like to achieve. For example, if you would like to have a certain qualification or complete a degree, be specific about what qualification or degree you would like to have. In addition, write down these goals in present tense, as if you have already achieved them.

Being specific gives your sub-conscious mind a a target. It is similar to setting a destination when planning a road trip. Do you want to drive to a particular park that has trails and a pool and is near a lake, or would you want to drive to just any park?

You might be wondering why we need to write goals in the present tense. There are two reasons. First, we can use these statements later as affirmations. (More on affirmations follows in the chapter "Step 5: Nailing it to the ground.") Second, by writing our goals as if they have already been realized, we activate a sort of energy of attraction that leads us toward the realization of our goals.

The Clearing Process

Many healers use the term *clearing process*. This process is used when we are not clear in our minds as to what we want, and, therefore, we are unable to manifest it. Goal-setting, putting your desires on a piece of paper or in a Word document, is a clearing process that gives you the clarity you need. It also sends a message to the Universe about what you really want. If you ask any one what they want, most of them will say, " million dollars". If you follow by another question as to what will they do with the million dollar, you would notice a pause or silence. This indicates that clarity is missing as to what they really want.

Have you ever had a situation where you are trying to listen to one radio station and another one is overlapping at the same time? This results in neither one of them being audible. Through our thoughts, we are continuously sending out messages to the Universe. When we are not clear, we are sending mixed messages. Result? nothing gets manifested or realized.

Clearing process cleans our thought processes and we start sending consistent messages out there. Thus, sooner rather than later, you will start to notice things happening in your life, where only a little effort on your part is needed to take you toward achieving your goals.

Another important note about goal-setting is that you can set whatever your heart desires for yourself or others; however, this and other exercises described in this book cannot be used to harm anyone in any way. That's not how the Universe works. Everything described in this book is related to clean, positive energy. Just as you cannot make a cloth dirty if you pour clean water on it, you cannot create negative results by using positive energy or its sources.

Does the Idea of Setting Goals Bore You?

What if you cannot convince yourself to do the goal-setting exercise in the first place? If you find it difficult to write your goals down, I suggest you visualize your goals. I discuss visualization in detail in the chapter "Step 3: Improving Your Self-Image," but following is a brief outline of how to do it.

Sit in a quiet place where you will not be disturbed for at least twenty minutes. Close your eyes and start counting backwards from 100. Focus on the numbers and try to imagine how each number looks as you count. You can imagine you are looking at a big number counter running backwards. Continue counting until you reach number one. When you are done, imagine yourself sitting with a piece of paper and a pen, or in front of a computer, writing down your goals. You don't have to go into detail, just imagine that you are calm, relaxed, and deeply interested in your task as you write down your life's goals.

Doing this visualization a couple of times should open you up for goal-setting and make it easier to go the next step.

To make it more interesting, cut out a picture from a newspaper or a magazine of some one sitting and writing something. Place your face cut out from one of your pictures onto the picture of person writing. You can create a similar image using image editing software as well.

The Process of Goal Setting

Sit in a quite area where you are sure you will not be disturbed for at least a few hours. You may be done sooner, but give yourself enough time, and do it when you are relaxed and not pressed for time and thinking that you have to go somewhere. Once you are settled, do the following:

- Close your eyes for a few minutes.
- Imagine that you have no limitations; you can do, have, or be whatever you want.
- Observe what comes to your mind when you are in this state.
- Try to keep your eyes closed and feel a sense of power.
- Gently bring yourself back to the room and write down everything that you imagined.

To free yourself from limiting thoughts, you can try imagining yourself with wings and flying, or you might imagine yourself swimming in water like a fish. Images such as these will liberate your thoughts, and you will be able to bring your real goals in life to the forefront of your mind.

I believe everyone has one overriding goal as their main purpose in life. If you don't already know what that purpose is, this exercise will help you realize it. All other goals are really steps to help you achieve that one main target. In my case, I always wanted to help people, but I also wanted to have enough money to support my family and those close to me. Through this goal-setting exercise, I realized that I could write books and give lectures to spread the word about this knowledge. At the same time, I have been able to earn enough money to support the people in my life whom I care for and live comfortably. What is your calling? Try to discover what it is. Why were you put on this earth?

If you find it difficult to find your true calling, spend some time trying to remember your childhood. When we were children, some of our activities brought us real joy; however, as we grow up, we lose those activities. We lose them because we don't have time for them. We have to earn money, we have family problems, we go through troubled times, and so on. When I was a young boy, I used to write stories. When I was writing those stories, I would really feel as if I was living them. It used to give me great joy. As life happened, I got busy with so many other things and stopped writing.

When I sat down to write my goals, I realized that I want to write again. It took me a few weeks, and then I was inspired to write an article. Once that was done, I was inspired to write a book. Now this book is a reality. I felt so much joy writing this book that cannot be explained in words. I truly believe that I have found my true calling. You can too. Go back to your childhood and try to find those things that used to bring you joy. Even if you had a troubled childhood, there was that one thing that would come out through all the negativity and pain. Try doing this and see if it helps you find your purpose in life.

Following are some suggestions for categories you can use when writing down your goals. You can add more if you wish.

- Personal growth
- Work/career

- Relationships
- Self-expression
- Money
- Lifestyle/possessions
- Leisure/travel

It's a good idea to break your goals into timeframes, such as one month, six months, one year, or five years. For example, a personal growth goal could be to register in one month's time at a college where you can take a course you need for certification in a certain technical field, and then to get certified in that field in one year.

While relaxing with your eyes closed and imagining that you are all-powerful and can achieve anything you want, it is important to identify feelings associated with, what you think are, your limitations. Often, when we think of our goals, we tend to come up with a million reasons why we cannot attain them.

In my own experience, every time I wrote down a goal, a number of negative thoughts about why I couldn't achieve it would come to me. I wrote down all my negative thoughts on a separate piece of paper. When you do this, don't stop, just write everything down. This is an excellent way to bring your limiting beliefs into the open. We will work more on negative thoughts in the chapters "Step 3: Improving Your Self-Image," "Step 4: Creative Imagination," and "Step 5: Nailing it to the ground."

> *"If you're bored with life—you don't get up every morning with a burning desire to do things—you don't have enough goals."*
>
> ~ Lou Holtz, American author and motivational speaker

Goal-Setting Categories

Personal Growth/Education

In this category, you will write what you have been thinking of doing regarding your education or personal growth, or both, but have not done so far,. These goals could be completing your education or getting certified in a particular technical field of your choice, or addressing a personal characteristic that you don't like. Perhaps you are too shy and find it difficult to mingle with people; alternatively, perhaps you have noticed that you are too outspoken and people try to avoid you.

Work/Career

One of the presenters in the movie *The Secret* discussed an incident where one of his clientscontacted him by email regarding a bad situation at his workplace. The presenter suggested that this person look at what he had written. His email was full of all the bad things that were happening at his workplace; it showed what was going on in the man's head. He was focusing only on the negative.

The point I am trying to make here is that in the work/career category, you write all the good that you want to happen in your work or career. Don't hold back. You can write what position you would like to achieve at work. If you have your own business, you can write the number of customers or the sales volume you would like to reach.

Relationships

I am sure that everyone would have something to write here. This is not restricted to spousal relationships; you can include your relationships with your parents, children, brothers, sisters, colleagues, friends, and so on. Write what is in your heart. If you have a son or daughter who has been out of touch, write down as a goal that he or she will visit or call you. If you are looking for a relationship that could lead to marriage, write it down as well. Remember to keep writing on a separate piece of paper, all the negative thoughts that keep telling you why you can't have what you want.

Self-Expression

This is where you can write how you would like to express yourself creatively. You may want to do something such as draw or paint in your leisure time, write a novel, or make professional-level videos and post them on YouTube. Listen to your inner voice and write down what it says.

Money

"Those who start with too little money are more likely to succeed than those who start with too much. Energy and imagination are the springboards to wealth creation."

~ Brian Tracy, Canadian author and motivational speaker

When writing their goals, people tend to dream big in all areas except money. In this category, don't write general statements such as "I am rich." Be more specific. Write down how much money you would like to have in the next five years. We often think, "If I did [such and such], I could make lots of money." Here you can write those plans as your goals.

An example of my own was when my Registered Education Savings Plan (RESP) for my daughter was not performing well. I had been concerned about it for some time. I wasn't satisfied with the agent I had been dealing with, so I wrote down that I would like to have a good agent who could advise me on the RESP and give me prompt responses. My existing agent had become unresponsive, so I got in touch with the institution's director, who assigned someone else to me, but he was inexperienced and I didn't want to deal with him, so I had the director assign someone else. Now I have a very experienced agent who is very professional and I am quite satisfied with the results.

Lifestyle/Possessions

This is where you can write about, for example, the car you would like to have, the jewelry you want, or how you would like to dress. I like to dress well, but I also do not like to spend too much money on the clothes. I wrote "I dress well" as one of my goals, and in a few weeks, I came to know that a particular brand name that I like had an outlet store near my house, where the clothes are almost always on sale. See how goals are realized!

Leisure/Travel

As the name suggests, this is where you write down the traveling you would like to do. It could be visiting Disney Land with your family, going to the Bahamas with the love of your life or going on an adventure tour. Let it all pour out!

Tracking Your Progress

If you have completed the exercise of writing down your goals, congratulations! If not, you might be going through the book just to see what else there is. That's fine. But do come back, write down your goals, and then take this next step and track your progress.

I created a tracking sheet to see how I was doing in attaining my goals. Keeping this sheet has a dual purpose. It gives you a great feeling when you see things happening that are leading to your goals. It also helps you focus your activities toward your goals. Following is my tracking sheet for my goal to bring my brother to Canada. You can customize your tracking sheet according to your goals. If you like, you could also add dates as your goals materialize.

- To have Karrar move out of Pakistan and come in Canada.
- I noticed an immigration firm had posted an update on the forum Pakistan Professionals. I wrote to them about Karrar.
- The immigration lawyer happens to be in Karachi and is willing to meet with Karrar in person.
- Karrar signed a contract with the immigration lawyer today.

- Karrar has received the list of documents he needs to submit.

- Today he submitted all his documents to the lawyer.

Step 3: Improving Your Self-Image

"Whatever your mind can conceive and believe, your mind can achieve."

~ Napoleon Hill (1883–1970), American new-thought author

Now that you have an understanding of how your mind works in response to various situations, and you have done the goal-setting exercises to discover what you would like to achieve in life, you are ready to move on to the next step and use this knowledge to change your life and realize your dreams.

What Is Self-Image?

Self-image is how you see yourself. There are people in this world who are well off but feel guilty about it. They may enjoy their work but see that their colleagues are miserable. They feel guilty about being happy and earning good money when others are not so blessed. Most of these thoughts stem from the belief that the Universe has limited resources, and, therefore, your wealth and happiness takes away what was meant for someone else.

Nothing could be further from the truth. I was having a chat with a friend of mine. He likes to give to charity, but he himself is not doing well financially. I said, "The only way you can help the poor even more is by having more money yourself. There's nothing wrong in having more money as long as it doesn't create artificial ego and pride and you treat others exactly the way you would like to be treated."

Feeling guilty for having been blessed indicates a low self-image. A low self-image is the number one reason why millions of people are uhappy. In almost all instances, a low self-image stems from beliefs we're fed from childhood. Following are some of these beliefs:

1. There is no easy way to succeed in life.
2. The harder I work, the more successful I will be.
3. The available resources are limited.
4. My family doesn't have enough money.
5. There isn't enough time.

6. My family has never owned a business; we were meant to do jobs for others.
7. Only the rich can have lots of money.
8. Rich people are bad.
9. You become rich by deceiving others.

You might have your own list of such negative beliefs that you were taught at home, in school, and by the media. Just the other day, I was switching channels and came across a program where a financial consultant was giving advice to families. She said, "For Christmas, I am giving you this jar. You can spend only what's in it." I thought, "Here we go again! Creating another limitation and that people will manifest physically.

In our society, we put too much emphasis on saving and very little on creating ways of earning more.

The Ego

Ego is an artificially created image in the mind of *me*. The mind says, "I am separate from others. I am superior to others, and if I bow down to someone else, I lose." As we have discussed, the mind is just a tool. Since we have given in to our minds and not tried to control it for so many years, we have created its own personality, which dictates our lives. To understand how the mind uses ego, lets look at an example. Two teenage sisters are planning to go to a party. Lets call them Sophy and Jennifer. They had both seen a particular dress in a store, and when they were discussing the party, Sophy said she was planning to buy the dress they had seen in the store. Jennifer said that she had been planning to buy that dress for the party. As a result, they ended up fighting, and their parents barred them from going to the party at all. Later on, Jennifer apologized to Sophy, and they became friends again after a brief chat.

This is what actually happened. Jennifer didn't really want the dress, but when Sophy said she wanted to buy it, Jennifer's ego came into play and she reacted spontaneously, without self-awareness; that is, without emotional intelligence.

Later on, Jennifer's true self, her higher self, came to the surface and she not only realized her mistake but apolized for it as well. Although Jennifer's ego existed, it had limited control over her.

How to Improve Your Self-Image

"Low self-esteem is like driving through life with your handbrake on."

~ Maxwell Maltz (1889–1975), American surgeon and self-help author

In his book *Psycho-Cybernetics*, Maxwell Maltz presents many examples of golfers who had felt the "winning feeling" just before winning a tournament. This is this feeling that we need to cultivate to be able to convert our dreams into reality. It can be described as conviction beyond a shadow of a doubt that you will attain a certain objective. There is no negative talk in the mind. In Pakistan, we have something called *mannat*, a vow to do something religious if a certain thing happens in our lives when we are faced with difficulties that are beyond our control.

We do mannat with the understanding that if the difficulty is resolved, we will do something called *niaz*, which is a kind of offering in the form of food, and then say some prayers to our God. When I was a child, in almost every instance whenever we did mannat, our problems were solved.

Without taking away the religious significance of these mannats, the principle at work is the same as that of the winning feeling. I am sure you must have had at least one incident in your life where you were sure that you would be successful, and you were. The problem is, we treat such events as isolated incidents and do not work on cultivating them into habitual patterns. We need to nurture that feeling and make it strong. But first, let's analyze the four behaviors that impact self-image and, in turn, our success: (1) gratitude, (2) judgmentalism, (3) complaining, and (4) trying to get more for less.

1. Gratitude

"Gratitude makes sense of our past, brings peace for today, and creates a vision for tomorrow."

~ Melody Beattie, American self-help author

Why is gratitude important in our journey to success? By saying thank you for the things we have been blessed with, we create within ourselves the belief that because good things have happened to us in the past, they will happen to us in the future. If we already have that belief, we make it stronger, and as it becomes stronger, our confidence in the number of good things that can happpen to us increases as well, and at the same time, our self-image improves.

The Universe does not burden us with anything that we are not capable of handling. This applies not only to the various tests we are put through but also to the good things in life. Many people dream of great things happening to them but lack the belief that their dreams will come true. Many people pray day in and day out for something, until one day they start to lose hope in their prayers, not realizing that the fault lies within, not without.

By saying "thank you, oh my creator, for this beautiful life," or saying thanks for all the things we possess, we acknowledge that good things can and will happen to us because they have already happened in the past. The Universe does not need us to say thank you. Our saying thank you is for ourselves, since it opens more doors, opportunities, and bounties for us. By thanking, we create within us the capability and capacity to receive more. This puts us in alignment with the plans of the Universe and unexpected good things start to show up.

How can we express Gratitude?

Generally, when we think of expressing gratitude, we think of saying thank you. However, there are other ways as well. Some of the examples are as follows:

At the Teller:

Often when you are at the checkout counter of a retail store like Walmart, Home Depot or McDonalds, the cashier asks the customer, "Would you like to donate a dollar for charity?" Have you noticed how many times people say no? People say no because what plays in their minds is that they have so little money themselves, how could they even think of parting with it. Well, I have news for you. That 'no' sends out a loud and clear message to the Universe that you believe in lack. You believe you have very little, will continue to have very little and by parting a dollar from that little money, you will be even more poor. The message being sent out to the Universe is "Give me less as I do not believe or expect to receive more, now or in the future".

In the workplace:

In an office environment, when a colleague asks another for help with something, what do you see happening? The other person says, "I have enough work of my own, so I can't help you out," but they are thinking, "Let him suffer, just like I suffered when I needed some help." What message do you think this sends to the Universe?

Anywhere else:

For instance, often when driving in the morning rush hour, another driver indicates that he or she wants to move into another lane, other drivers will not give way. What plays in their heads might go like this: "I am already so late. I cannot give way to him or it will delay me even further." In reality, when traffic is moving at a snail's pace, it does not really matter if you are one car behind. It will make only a fraction of a second's difference. By refusing to give way, we again confirm our belief to the Universe that there is lack of time, and thus lack of time is what comes to us. If you read lives of some of the renowned people in this world, many of them died at a young age but were able to achieve so much. There are others who live to full 80 years of age, when they die, there is nothing left by them but a name on the tomb stone. Those who believe in abundance of time just like any other resource, are able to do so much in a short period of time. Those who keep sending the message of lack, die with no trace.

If you fill your car's gas tank because the price of fuel is expected to go up a few cents the next day, does it really make much difference? People go crazy about filling their tanks. This is instigated by the belief that we do not have enough money, so we get more today because we have no faith in what will be tomorrow. If you think about it, how long will that full tank last? It will be empty again soon. We need to shift our belief that we live in a Universe of lack to one in which we live in a Universe of abundance.

Many religions of the world advocate meeting others with a smile. It is considered a form of charity as well. The following quotation is an example:

"When you smile to your brother's face, it is charity."
~ Prophet Muhammad (peace be upon him), mentioned in the books *Sunan al-Tirmidhî* (1879) *Sahîh Ibn Hibbân* (475 and 530) and *Musnad al-Bazzâr*.

When you give a dollar or a dime or a small amount of time for a good cause, or when you help others in their chores, you send out the message that you believe there is more. You believe in the abundance of nature. As the famous saying goes, "Actions speak louder than words."

I am not advocating that you should contribute

everything to charity or spend hours helping someone while your own work suffers. But every once in a while, do give away some of your time, money, or knowledge when someone asks. Some times even when no one asks but you can see they can use some kind of help.

The key point to remember is doing good for others is a win/win situation. When we do soemthing for others, we touch that person deeply. Plus, we send out a positive message to the Universe which in turn manifests our dreams.

Business world is plagued by the feeling that one person has to lose for others to win. Many business deals often break down since one party did not agree to certain concession for the other. This can be changed if competitors look at each other as sharing the same customers rather than focussing on how to drive the other out of business.

2. Judgmentalism

"Judgements prevent us from seeing the good that lies beyond appearances."

~ Wayne Dyer, American self-help author and lecturer

In modern society, being judgemental about others is seen as a bad thing. It can certainly influence our self-image and success in life. The problem is, we have identified the problem and so we try to avoid doing it openly, but we continue to do it in our minds. For example, a stranger might walk into a gathering and we immediately start judging the person. First, we look at the their dress and style and try to assess how wealthy they are, and we are judgemental not only about the person's financial situation but also about whether or not he or she is a nice person. In most cases, we form a negative impression. If we do get to talk to the person, we don't give them the opportunity to prove themselves because we go into the conversation with a predetermined opinion based on the person's appearance. This is all happening in our minds, without any information to support those opinions.

We are also judgmental about people based on the opinions of others and on gossip. We rarely investigate the truth of these opinions and gossip. We seldom ask those who are being judgmental as to why they said what they said about the other person.

Another closely related habit emanating from being judgemental is backbiting. Backbiting reveals our own low self-image and sense of inferiority. Since we feel inferior, we talk badly of others to create the illusion that we are better than them—that we are superior. This is likely the reason in almost all the circumstances as to why people backbite.

Being negatively judgemental about others based on their appearance or what you have heard from others can often deprive you of an excellent relationship or a great resource that could contribute to your success in life, emotionally and financially. If you really want to achieve your goals, see all others as an extension of yourself. Give them a fair chance and never judge them unless you have personally dealt with them.

Even then, if you don't like something another person says or does, ask them to explain rather than try to figure out the reason yourself. Others, just like you, have their own challenges, and sometimes they don't even realize what they have done to offend you unless you bring it to their attention.

Following is an example of a journal you can keep to track your judgemental behavior about people. Write in it whenever you meet a new person or feel bad about a particular situation.

Judgmental-Behavior Journal

Date	Incident	Judgmental thought	What did I do?	My findings
31/03/13	Julie did not show up at my wedding rehearsal despite my repeated reminders.	She thinks she is too busy with her life. I am her best friend, and she can't even give me a few hours of her time.	I spoke to her about it after the rehearsal.	She had an unexpected deadline to meet at work and her cell phone battery had run out, and by the time it was recharged, it was too late to call.

This is just one example to give you an idea. You can see the difference between what your mind came up with and reality.

I am not saying that you will always find an answer that makes perfect sense. For instance, in the above example, you might actually have found that Julie didn't feel like going to the rehearsal and she was too ashamed to call you. We are all human. We enter into as well as get out of relationships. What we do not do is communicate. We are judgmental and react based on our ill-supported conclusions, and then blame it on life.

3. Complaining

"If you took one-tenth the energy you put into complaining and applied it to solving the problem, you'd be surprised by how well things can work out..."

~ Randy Pausch (1960–2008), American author and professor of computer science and human-computer interaction

This brings us to the next behavior that can impact your self-image, and thus your success: complaining. You must have noticed how people all around you complain about one thing or another. It can feel good to complain. But there is a problem: The way life works, complaining only gives you more to complain about.

When you complain, you affirm things in life that you do not want. You will learn about affirmations in the chapter "Step 5: Nailing it to the ground," but here is a brief explanation: Affirmations are statements about a certain aspect of, or goal in, your life that you say every day. The purpose of affirmations is to create ideas within your subconscious mind, that will lead you toward your goals.By complaining, we basically affirm those things in life that we do not want.The solution is simple: Whenever you find something to complain about, try to think of a way to change whatever it is you are complaining about. If it cannot be changed, try to find the best way to live through it. Have you ever heard the saying, "The brightest sun is just behind the darkest clouds"?

Just imagine, if Edison had complained about how unsuccessful he was in his attempts to create a light bulb, would we have light bulbs today? A business reality television series in Canada called *Dragon's Den*, based on a Japanese program called *Money Tiger*, and now being produced worldwide (the American version is *Shark Tank*), features entrepreneurs who present their business ideas in order to secure investors from the program's panel of venture capitalists. In many cases, you see entrepreneurs who saw a problem, came up with a solution for it, and eventually made hundreds of thousands of dollars from it. Would they have done anything of the sort if they had stopped at complaining about the problem? In short, complaining works against your dreams; it negatively affects self-image and thus ensures that you stay in the same loop forever.

Step 4: Creative Imagination

"Millions of people are concentrating daily on poverty and failure and getting both in overabundance"
~ Wanjala Mshila and Grace Obado, authors of *The Law of Success: Adapted for Africa*, based on the work of Napoleon Hill

What Is Creative Imagination or Visualization?

In 1977, José Silva published a book called *The Silva Mind Control Method*. In this excellent book, José Silva, who did research on and participated in various scientific studies on mind control, describes how our minds can influence our lives.

One such influence is the ability to heal our bodies with the help of our minds. An explanation for this was given by Ernest Rossi in his book *The Psychobiology of Mind-Body Healing: New Concepts of Therapeutic Hypnosis*, where he explained that most healing using hypnosis is the result of the mind influencing blood flow, which leads to changes in the body.

An example of the mind controlling the body was

demonstrated in studies with meditators and non-meditators to learn if it is possible for people to learn to control their body temperature. It was shown that meditators in a Himalayan ceremony in Tibet could increase their body temperature in frigid weather and dry wet sheets that were wrapped around their naked bodies. The researchers concluded if people meditated using a technique called "forceful breath," they could learn to regulate their body temperatures, and with visualization, they could sustain the increased temperature for longer period.[4]

Various techniques for mind control have been developed. One particularly powerful technique is known as visualization, which we touched on in the chapter "Step 2: Unleashing the Genie."

---

[4] Maria Kozhevnikov et al., "Neurocognitive and Somatic Components of Temperature Increases during g-Tummo Meditation: Legend and Reality," *Public Library of Science One* 8, no. 3 (2013): e58244, doi:10.1371/journal.pone.0058244, www.plosone.org/article/info%3Adoi%2F10.1371%2Fjournal.pone.0058244.

"Creative visualiation is the technique of using your imagination to create what you want in your life."

~ Shakti Gawain, American new-age author

In simple terms, visualizaton is like creating a movie in your mind that shows your ideal outcome, and then feeling it as if it were happening right now.

What Role Does Visualization Play in the Realization of Our Dreams?

You may find the discussion of visualization difficult to digest, especially if you are used to looking at the world from the point of view of "scientific proof." You may think that I am talking fairy tales.

Well, here is something that might spark your interest. If you can, try to get your hands on a documentary entitled *Something Unknown Is Doing We Don't Know What*. This documentary is a compilation of scientific research that proves how powerful our minds are and how thoughts can influence material objects.

Studies also show how people can communicate with each other even though they are not facing each other or speaking to one another. Consider the Brain-Computer Interfacing (BCI) experiment *B2B – BrainToBrain: A BCI Experiment*.[5] In this experiment, conducted by Dr. Christopher James at the University of Southampton's Institute of Sound and Vibration Research, one person communicates his thoughts (in the form of binary numbers on the computer) over the Internet to another person's computer, which transmits the numbers to that person's brain via the flashing of an LED lamp.[6] The communication was generated by brain power only.

There is no doubt that the role our thoughts play in our lives has been proved beyond any doubt. With those doubts now clear, let's do some visualizations.

---

[5] James Christopher, B2B – *BrainToBrain: A BCI Experiment* (May 2009), YouTube video, 3:25, https://www.google.ca/#q=Christopher+James+BCI.
[6] University of Southampton, "Brain-Computer Interface Allows Person-to-Person Communication through Power of Thought," *Science Daily* (October 6, 2009), www.sciencedaily.com/releases/2009/10/091006102637.htm.

I have designed five steps in the process of visualizing: (1) creating focus, (2) rating what you want, (3) imagining a scene, (4) feeling it, and (5) letting go and having faith.

A good resource for a detailed understanding of how to create movies in your mind is a book by Adelaide Bry entitled *Visualization: Directing the Movies of Your Mind.*

A Few Notes on Visualization Practice

If you have never done visualization and would like to practice it before doing it for your goals, you can do this three-step exercise:

1. Relaxation

Find a comfortable place and lie down. Close your eyes and take slow, deep breaths. Begin by bringing your attention to your body. First, focus on your feet and let them relax. Then feel the relaxation moving slowly up your legs. Imagine they are sinking into the floor or the bed as they relax. Continue to slowly move your focus further up your body. Feel your hips, stomach, and lower back relax, and then move up and feel your chest and back relaxing, then, slowly and gradually, your shoulders, arms, and hands become totally relaxed. Then let your neck relax, then all the muscles in your face. Feel your eyes relax, and your scalp. Now you are in a state of total relaxation. During this process, if any other thoughts come to your mind, let them pass through. Try to give your full attention to relaxing your body.

2: The Journey

Once you are relaxed and focused, imagine that you are a bird flying high in the sky. You are flying at a comfortable speed, and you can feel your feathers fluttering in the cool but pleasant air. It's a bright day and you can see everything clearly. You hear an airplane above you. You look up and see that it is huge, and there is a red flag on its tail fin. You also see its wheels folded into the fuselage. Imagine that the plane causes the air to push you and make you fly faster. You also hear the cars below, and you see them, in various colors, driving along the roads and streets. Some of them are stopped at traffic lights. You also hear children playing in a park just beneath you. You see them playing with a ball, laughing, and talking. Some of them are looking up at you. You see other birds flying by you as well. Finally, you land on a branch of a tree to relax. You feel tired after all that flying. You close your eyes just for a moment.

3. The Return

To end the visualization exercise, slowly open your eyes and come back to the room. Try to remember all the things you saw and write the details down on a piece of paper.

There are no rules to visualization. Some people have vivid imaginations and can create scenes in great detail. Others may only be able to hear the sounds of the scenes they create, whereas some may only be able to feel their creations, without really seeing them. Whatever form your visions take, they are all okay. The key is to try to imagine something!

Creating Focus

"Imagination is more important than knowledge."

~ Albert Einstein (1879–1955), German theoretical physicist

Now that you have practiced visualization, let's apply it to your goals. The first step in being able to create a movie in your mind is to stop your mind's constant chatter so that you can focus. You may have noticed that every day, from the time you get up from your bed, there is constant chatter going in your head. My daughter is four years old, and we play nursery rhymes for her. One day she asked my wife, "Mama can you hear it? The song is playing in my head." My wife smiled and said, "No, baby, I cannot hear it."

Though no one else can hear what's playing in our minds, we certainly can. Millions of people think that it is a normal part of living. I have news for them. It's not. Continuous, uncontrolled chatter going on in our minds chokes us. So what can we do about it? The ability to control what goes in our minds and create silence when we desire it has been practiced by great spiritual leaders for all time. It can be difficult to do in the beginning, but it's not impossible.

Being able to silence the internal chatter is important for visualization. If you are not able to stop this ongoing buzz, creating images in your mind with full focus will be extremely difficult. Following are some suggestions on how you can try to create silence in your mind.

The Door-Shutting Technique

For this exercise, lie down and close your eyes. Relax and imagine that your mind is like a small house. There is a living room, where a lot of clutter has piled up; these are the thoughts that come to your mind, thoughts such as an interview you have the next day, an argument you had with your spouse, work deadlines, money problems, friendship woes, anxiety about exams, loss of a family member, health concerns, bad decisions you made, or office politics. What you first have to do is label these thoughts as related to past or worrisome events. For example, if you have a job interview the next day and you are worried about how it will go, imagine yourself opening the door to a room marked "Worries," and let the thoughts relating to that interview slide into that room, and then close the door. On the other hand, if you had an argument with your spouse and the scene of the argument and the uncomfortable feelings associated with it start playing again in your mind, imagine yourself now opening the door to a room called "Past," and let those thoughts and feelings move into that room, and then close the door. Eventually, all the thoughts that race through your mind and prevent you from focusing can be put in a room behind closed doors so that your mind is clear. Some situations may be more difficult to do this with than others, but all that is needed is practice.

The Counting Technique

With your eyes closed, breathe deeply and then start slowly counting backwards from one hundred. Try to focus on the numbers as you count, and continue to breathe deeply; this will help you to relax your body and your mind. The key to this exercise is to imagine what each number looks like as you count backwards. I imagine the numbers being displayed one by one on a billboard. Various thoughts will try to come in, but let them slide away and keep your focus on the numbers. With some practice, you should have a clear mind by the time you reach number one.

The Focus Technique

This is another technique that I use. I sit down, ensuring my spine is straight by supporting it with a pillow or against something hard, such as a wall. I close my eyes and start breathing deeply and slowly. I then focus on a sound. This could be the ticking of a clock, the noise of a fan, or water trickling in an aquarium. Thoughts do come, but I try to keep my focus on the sound. After a while, the thoughts start to become faint. My body is relaxed and I repeat in my mind, "I am going deeper and deeper into my mind." This is the stage when I start creating the visualization of my desired goals.

Calming your mind is an achievement on its own. Practice is most important for this step. Once you have reached that deeper level, the feeling in itself is very comforting. There are many benefits of being able to shut your train of thoughts, even if it is for ten to twenty minutes a day. If you continue doing it, you will notice your ability to concentrate during various activities will improve. Your memory will also improve tremendously, which will help you improve your self-image. You will become more self-aware, and your emotional intelligence will improve, all of which will contribute to your reaching your goals and improving your life.

Rating What You Want

In the exercise on goal-setting in the chapter "Step 2: Unleashing the Genie," I had you write down all the goals that came to your mind. While you were writing your goals, you were also writing the negative thoughts that came to your mind about why you couldn't achieve those goals. Now is the time to use those thoughts and give them a positive spin through visualization.

Following are a few examples of how to convert your negative thoughts and beliefs into positive ones. You will also find more examples in, "Step 5: Nailing it to the ground."

Converting the Negative into the Positive

Negative Thoughts/Beliefs	Positive Spin
No one in my family has ever had their own business.	There is always a first time.
My wish to have my own	My parents will be very

business will upset my parents.	proud of my success.
I have no confidence at all.	I have confidence in my abilities.
Anything I say or do will be ridiculed, and I will be made fun of.	Universe will bring success to me.
I cannot afford to get higher education.	I have resources available to get the education that I desire.
I am too fat to be attractive to anyone.	I have a charming personality and people like to hang around with me.
I will never be able to pay off this debt.	I am financialy independent. Wealth comes to me easily and effortlessly.
I have had weight issues all my life. I can't control it.	I am a healthy person. I can feel vibrant energy flowing through my body.

Notice that you don't repeat the negative words in the

positive spin. For example, you don't say, "My parents will not be upset." You give a positive touch to the full sentence. The more you repeat positive, feel-good words, the more they stay in your subconscious mind. Note that I said *feel*-good words. It's not enough just to *say* these statements; you need to *feel* as if these statements were true.

Use the chart above to list all your negative feelings that came up in the goal-setting exercise. Once you are done, convert these negative beliefs into positive statements, and then rate them based on which ones make you feel better than the others. For instance, the statement "I have resources available to get the education that I desire" may make you feel much better than the other statements, so rate it as number one. Do this for all the positive statements. Some might feel the same, so you can give those ones the same number.

The purpose of rating is to organize which goal will help your self-image to improve more quickly, and therefore, which one you'll use to visualize first. There are no hard-and-fast rules; it's your life, and you can decide what's best. These are just indicators you can use to help you decide more easily. It can be helpful if, before visualizing your goal, you write down what you would like to see and feel when your desire is realized.

Imagining a Scene

"Everything comes to us that belongs to us if we create the capacity to receive it."

~ Rabindranath Tagore (1861–1941), Bengali poet

This is the fun part. It's time to enjoy. Get into a relaxed state, and when you are almost relaxed and focused, think about the number one desire from the rating exercise above.

Now imagine that you have already realized your goal and are now seeing the results. In this visualization exercise, you would imagine yourself in a scene, you imagine yourself enjoying the achievements and create that scene in your mind.

If your goal is to get a particular job, imagine yourself sitting in front of the interviewer, and she is saying to you, "Congratulations, Mr. Jacob, we have decided to offer you the job." If your goal is to win something, picture yourself checking the results of the contest and finding that you have won. Feel the emotions associated with this scene, and I mean really feel the excitement of the happy moment!

If you prefer to visualize several goals at once, that's fine too. For example, you might imagine that you are driving the car of your dreams and sitting next to you is the love of your life. You are the artist here, and the canvas is blank. Fill it with colors and sketches of your life to be.

Do Not Focus Your Visualization on the "How"

Try to visualize only the realization of your goal. In the example of the job interview above, try not to visualize the questions being asked in the interview going well. Similarly, if you are looking to buy a car, don't imagine that you got a raise or won money in the lottery as the reason why you can buy the car. Focus your imagination on creating the scene of having what you desire. Focus on the end result. Leave the domain of *how* to the Universe. The Universe has unlimited resources at its disposal. Once you are in alignment with the Universe, it will give you what you ask for, and, even better, in the best possible way.

Feeling It

I often wondered what the difference is between me and my creator regarding creation. Well, my conclusion is simple. What I create has no life. By this I mean that if I were to paint a flower or carve a sculpture of an animal, it will never have life. The Universe, on the other hand, gives life to its creations. That's the real difference.

"Your ability to manifest something in life is possible only when you can give feelings to your imagination. Without feelings, imagination is like a painting or a sculpture with no life."

~ Zeeshan Raza

Everyone has attained some success in life. It helps if you can revisit how you felt when you had achieved those successes. It's a matter of rejuvenating those feelings; however, this time you will do it with the intention of attaining your desires. *You* are now in control!

In the example above with the interviewer who is congratulating you on being hired for the job, you need to feel the scene as if it were really happening. Try to bring yourself to that scene with your entire being. How would it feel when she shakes your hand? Imagine the feeling in your hand. Feel the rush of excitement when she congratulates you—the adrenaline rush through your body. The best of actors on film and stage are those who can go into the character, feel it, and then play it.

When you imagine yourself driving the car of your dreams with the love of your life, feel the air going through your hair as you drive through beautiful scenery. Feel your hands on the steering wheel, your legs switching between the accelerator and brakes. Feel the presence of your loved one. What would it feel like to be sitting next to him or her? Hear his or her voice as they talk to you in a loving way.

Let Go and Have Faith

"Faith is taking the first step even when you don't see the whole staircase."

~ Martin Luther King Jr. (1929–1968), American activist and leader of the Civil Rights Movement

A long time ago, there was a saint. People used to go to his grave to pray for their desires. Almost everyone got what they wanted. There was a blind man who went there for several days. One day, he was sitting and praying for sight, when the king of the land arrived. The king asked the blind man how long he had been coming to visit the grave of the saint. The blind man replied that it had been about a week, and the king said, "If you don't get your sight by tomorrow when I come here again, I will chop your head off." The blind man was very worried. His quest had become a matter of life or death. The next day when the king returned, the blind man's eyesight was restored. He was able to see again.

What happened? When the blind man began to pray, he

must have had doubts. When we are doubtful about whether our goals will be achieved, we seldom achieve them. When restoring his eyesight through prayers became a matter of life or death, the blind man must have placed full confidence in his prayers, and so he regained his sight.

The last step in successful visualization is to let go and have faith. Nothing in this world can ever be achieved if we don't believe it will happen.

I can understand that the concept of visualization and turning daydreams into reality might seem to some people to not be practical or serious. However, I would still stress that you please give it a try. You are not paying anyone for this, and you may spend hours sitting in front of the TV watching programs created by others.Why not watch programs that you create for yourself? For one, they will make you feel great. Secondly, you might actually start to see changes in your life—changes that you never thought would take place.

The best way to develop your faith is to visualize about smaller objectives. For example, visualize about what your wife/husband/boyfriend/girlfriend/mom/dad will make you for lunch on the weekend. Imagine something that you love to eat. Don't tell him or her about it. It is more likely than not that it will happen. Since it's a small thing, tell your mind you want to give it a try to avoid negative comments such as "it's not going to work." You have nothing to lose, and you won't be too attached to the goal.

What's Big? What's Small?

An important point worth mentioning is that many people are highly successful in realizing dreams about smaller things, such as a cup of tea, their favorite meal, or even a parking spot, but when it comes to things that their minds perceive as big, they fail. Why is it that you can visualize and get a parking spot right in front of the door, but you are unable to land that big customer account or get that car of your dreams?

The reason is that we hold very strong limiting beliefs about life and how things work. The Universe has all the resources at its disposal. We read in magazines and newspapers that America has more millionaires today than there were a decade ago. What this means is that more people have been able to attract wealth into their lives. We also hear stories about people recovering from life-threatening diseases, and yet we cannot comprehend that such success could to come to us. For the Universe, nothing is too big or too small. The fault lies in our own beliefs, where we perceive things to be big or small. The Universe provides those who expect to live their lives from hand to mouth with just enough resources to do this. Others, who believe that the Universe provides abundance, get abundance in money, health, relationships, and more.

In situations where our limiting beliefs are holding us back from our desires, such as "success is very difficult to achieve" or "I could never have such an expensive car," we need to do what is called *clearing*.

Clearing

Clearing means just that—to clear. The purpose of clearing is to clear our old, restricting beliefs about ourselves and our abilities and replace them with new, enabling beliefs. Clearing can be done in two steps: (1) visualizations, and (2) affirmations.

1. Visualizations for Clearing

In his book *The Attractor Factor: 5 Easy Steps for Creating Wealth*, Joe Vitale provides the following exercise, attributed to one of the masters of the Law of Attraction, Bob Proctor, to clear ourselves of our old beliefs.

Take two pieces of paper (for this exercise, it is better to write with hands, as writing provides more impact). On one piece of paper, write down all the negative emotions or thoughts that come to your mind about a goal or subject. For example, "I have limited finances," "I am always living hand to mouth," "I can hardly pay off my bills," or "I have nothing left to enjoy in life after my expenses are paid."

Now close your eyes and start to feel the way you do when you are faced with this situation. You might feel like crying. Try to get into the emotions associated with each statement. Feel the emotions, and then let them pass through. If you don't feel much, ask yourself over and over: "How do I normally feel when I am faced with this situation or when I am worried about it?" The repetition should eventually bring the feeling out.

After five to ten minutes you will probably have felt the emotions, which will eventually bring you a sense of calm. If you shed some tears, you will soon feel a sense of release. Now open your eyes and write down what you desire on the second piece of paper. For example, "I want wealth in abundance," "I want to feel relaxed when I look at my bank account because I have plenty to pay my expenses, with even more to save and spend," "I want money to come to me with ease," or "I want to be rich and relaxed." You can go on and describe in detail as much as you would like.

Now take the paper containing your negative feelings, tear it up, and throw it away. This symbolizes that those feelings have no place in your life anymore. Take the other paper with your positive feelings and keep it with you.

2. *Affirmations for Clearing*

I will discuss affirmations in more detail in the chapter "Step 5: Nailing it to the ground," but for the sake of our clearing exercise, take what you just wrote as your desire for clearing and turn it into an affirmation. For example, instead of saying, "I want wealth in abundance," you would write, "I have wealth in abundance." Close your eyes again and visualize your desire. Go into the good feeling as if it were already happening. See yourself enjoying this wealth and feeling relaxed.

If the clearing exercise isn't working for you, you might need to do it once a week for two or three weeks. If you still have problems, rethink what you are working on. Maybe there is a different issue that is bothering you that you should be focusing on instead. An example could be if your spouse keeps complaining about a lack of money, when you evidently have enough, then it's your relationship with your spouse that you need to work on, not money problems.

You can use the clearing exercise not only to replace negative with positive beliefs but also to clarify what you need in a particular situation. In addition, what if you cannot push yourself to sit down and write your goals? Here is an idea: Take two pieces of paper. On the first, describe your current situation; for example, "I am stuck in a nine-to-five job that I hate. When I come back home, I have nothing to do except watch TV. My weekends are wasted because there is nothing interesting to do. Life is passing me by and I'm not getting anywhere." Next, close your eyes and feel the emotions associated with these thoughts.

Even if you haven't thought about what you would like to do, in almost all instances, those ideas and thoughts are sitting in your subconscious mind. However, due to the negative clutter we collect, we prevent those bright ideas from coming forward. So, take the second piece of paper and start writing whatever thoughts come to your mind about your future. By doing this, you are clearing the negative from your mind and making way for your future to come to the forefront. You should find that you feel great just by writing these positive thoughts.

Do not force anything. Just sit and let your thoughts flow in. It may not work on your first attempt, so you might have to try clearing the negative thoughts once more, perhaps in a week's time, and then try writing your future again. If you really want to change the way things are, this will work.

Forgiveness

"To forgive is to set a prisoner free and discover that the prisoner was you."

~ Lewis B. Smedes (1921–2002), American Christian author, ethicist, and theologian

Almost everyone who has had a bad experience with someone ends up feeling bad in their heart. This can be a big fight with your best friend, someone who cheated you with money, or even an encounter with one of your family members. They start living with that feeling and never address it. How do you deal with such a situation?

The best way is through forgiveness.

Forgiveness is not "forgive and forget." That is not helpful. If you really want to feel calm within yourself, real forgiveness is required. By real forgiveness, I mean having no negative thoughts or feelings at all about the other. For example, a brother and sister I know live with their spouses and kids in two different cities. Years earlier, they had a fight about some issue and stopped talking. One day, I asked the brother if he was still mad at his sister. He said, "She is happy in her life and I have forgiven her and am busy with my own life." You can immediately read into this statement that the negative sentiment is still there, even though he said he had forgiven her. In fact, he had not.

Visualization can also be used to forgive people and rid yourself of the negative emotions associated with the conflict you have with someone.

Close your eyes and bring yourself to the state of focus we talked about in visualization. Imagine that you are sitting in front of the person you have negative feelings toward. Tell them that you no longer feel that way about them. Say that you have forgiven them and ask for forgiveness in return. Then tell them they can now go on their way. Feel that you are releasing any negative feelings within you about the person. If you still feel resentment within you, you might need to do this a few more times. When you do this for someone with whom you were close, such as your parents, spouse, partner, or siblings, you might find yourself becoming quite emotional. In an exercise such as this, becoming emotional indicates that you are doing it correctly.

Step 5: Nailing it to the ground

"Affirmative statements are going beyond the reality of the present into the creation of the future through the words you use in the now."

~ Louise Hay, American motivational author

The final step in this process is using affirmations. Affirmations and visualization go hand in hand, and they work like magic when done simultaneously.

Affirmation literally means "firming something up." Visualizations help you create an idea in your imagination while your eyes are closed. Affirmations are done with open eyes to bring those ideas from thoughts to reality.

Affirmations cannot be considered lies to yourself. You are creating the future that you desire in your thoughts and transforming it into reality. This is the sketch, the draft that you are giving to the Universe, which will give you either exactly what you are looking for or something even better.

When we make affirmations, we repeat a statement or a

series of statements. Ideally, they should be done once in the morning, just after you wake up, and once in the evening, just before you go to bed. Your mind is in the best state at these times to receive new ideas and to plant the seeds for your future life. Many spiritual teachings and religions encourage prayers at these times as well.

It's best to do affirmations while standing in front of a mirror and looking right in your eyes. It might be difficult in the beginning. You might feel that you are making a fool of yourself by talking to yourself, or you might feel uncomfortable looking into your own eyes and making these statements. Feeling uneasy while doing this the first few times is not uncommon. If you should feel this way, there is nothing to worry about. The trick is to stick with it. After a while, you will start to enjoy it.

You can also write down your affirmations in bold letters on sticky notes and place them throughout your house or in certain places in your office where you can see them during the day, such as on your refrigerator, near your computer in your home office, or even on the bathroom mirror. If you are someone like me who drinks a lot of water, each visit you make to the bathroom will trigger those positive, happy thoughts and accomplish the clearing exercise you learned in the previous chapter, "Step 3: Improving Your Self-Image." My method is to type my affirmations in different colors on the computer, and then print them on colored paper and cut them into small squares and place them everywhere. Here is an example:

I am happy ☺, healthy, rich and relaxed. I have lots of extra money and lots of extra time for myself and my family.

I try to use soothing, light colors and avoid harsher, dark colors such as red, which can convey negative feelings that prevent your affirmations from serving their purpose. You can even print them in black and white.

Another idea is to use these statements as your computer's screensaver. You can leave the laptop/desktop switched on so that when the screensaver is activated, your subconscious mind can get these messages throughout the day. You can also make a PowerPoint presentation and keep it in your phone. Play them first thing in the morning when you wake up and in the evening before going to sleep.

There are some free-wares (free softwares) which run in the background while you are working on your computer. They have tons of affirmations already programmed. You can select topicsyou would like to focus on. This could be health, finances, happiness etc. You could add your own affirmations as well. When running, these softwares display various affirmations for a fraction of the second on the screen. These are displayed for such a short time that you will not notice them and it will not interrupt your work. However, your sub-conscious mind will read it. Repetition being the key, the idea is you will be communicating a certain set of affirmations again and again to your sub-conscious mind.

You can also put up various powerful affirmations in photo frames at different places of your home.

You can come up with your own ideas; there are no hard-and-fast rules.

The underlying aim is to register these statements deep inside your brain. We are surrounded by negativity everywhere. The goal should be to replace that with positivity.

See what works best for you.

Affirmations can be used for two purposes:

1. To reinforce a goal that you are currently working on through visualization.

2. To replace your deep-seated negative thoughts with positive ones and create a general state of happiness in your everyday life.

Reinforcing a Goal

An affirmation for a particular goal can be explained like this: Imagine you are interested in getting a particular car. Let's say you have visualized a Jaguar 2014 F-Type. Your affirmation can take the following shapes:

- "I love driving my new Jaguar 2014 model. I love its black color and enjoy the smooth driving pleasure it gives me."

- "I now own the F-Type Jaguar and am in awe of the fun I have while driving it."

If you don't understand how this works, it doesn't mean it doesn't work. Positive thoughts have much more power than negative ones as long as such thoughts are expressed with emotions. In other words, you don't just make statements; you actually feel the associated emotions of realizing those dreams.

When I am working on a certain project, I use the following affirmations and repeat them in my mind as many times during the day as possible. If I get negative thoughts about that particular project, I immediately replace them with any or all of the following, filling in the blank with whatever project you are working on:

- "I have complete faith that the Universe will help me manifest success in my _____ project."
- "I am surrounded by the people, circumstances, and resources necessary to successfully execute my _____ project."
- "My actions are in alignment with the universal plan. I can see my dream of _____ coming to reality."

Generating a Positive Perspective

Every second of our lives, our minds keep chattering. We think we have no control over this. An interesting phenomenon about our brains is that they can think only one thought at a time. If you are really interested in changing your life, you need to be in charge of your thoughts. This is achievable; however, it does require practice. If you have already practiced the exercise in the chapter "Step 1: You've Got the power" you will be aware of your own emotions and thinking patterns. I would like to emphasize, however, that once you have become expert at this, it won't stay with you forever. You have to continue practicing the meditations and other activities suggested in this book. For instance, if you stop doing visualizations or making positive affirmations, your mind will slowly go back to its negative thinking patterns. This is simply because we are surrounded by negativity from various sources throughout the day.

Now is the time to start taking control and changing those thinking patterns. In the table below, I have taken just a few of the negative thoughts that our minds create and given them a positive spin. You can choose the ones that appeal to you most. I recommend you use these affirmations every day of your life. The best way to choose them is to say each one a couple of times and notice which ones make you feel better and which ones have no effect. Use the ones that make you feel relaxed and at peace. Once you have an idea of how this works, you can expand on it and create your own.

Changing Negative Thoughts into Affirmations

Negative Thoughts	Affirmations
I hate going to this job every day.	• Another beautiful day has come and interesting challenges await me at work.
I am terrible at resolving problems.	• Solutions come to me with little effort. • People appreciate my problem-solving skills. • Problems have a way of leading to solutions easily and effortlessly.
I am in a bad mood today.	• I feel great this morning.

	• It's a pleasant day, and I have lots of energy.
I am going to be late.	• I will reach my destination well before I need to be there.
I have a big bill/payment coming up, and I don't know how I'll manage it.	• God/the Universe/Allah/Spirit has given me prosperity and wealth in abundance.
I feel sick every day.	• I feel great energy flowing through my body. • I am in perfect health. • I am glowing with happiness and vitality. • I love life and am happy to be alive.
My salary/pay/wage is too low.	• I am now willing to receive income from multiple sources. • I am now open to receive sufficient income from various sources

That task is too difficult for me.	• I am a capable person and can successfully deliver on any task assigned to me.
It's very difficult to deal with [person's name].	• I am surrounded by people who appreciate me as a person and are easy to deal with. • Everyone I deal with looks after my best interests. • People love me and I love them. • When I need someone to do something, they do it with a smile. • People cooperate with me and willingly help me to reach my goals.
I'm too busy/I have no time.	• I easily complete my assignments on time.

	• I am able to manage deadlines in the most effective manner, and I am in control all the time. • I am blessed with plenty of time, so I can do many things harmoniously. • Timing works for me, and things get done with plenty of time to spare. • I have a wealth of time, which allows me to get things done efficiently and effectively. • I always have a wealth of time, and I complete my tasks in a relaxed and controlled manner.
I'm too old.	• I am growing more energetic and vibrant every day. • With the passage of years, my increased knowledge helps me

	do more things in life.
	• I feel young at heart and enriched in spirit every day of my life.
I don't have anyone to go with.	• I attract people who bring happiness to my life. • People like to be around me and enjoy my company. • I have friends and family who support me in every step of my life.
This hurts, that hurts, I hurt.	• My body is always doing its best, and I stay in great health. • I feel powerful, positive energy flowing through every part of my body. • Every inch of my body, my muscles, and my bones are relaxed and at ease.

I'm too out of shape.	• I love my body, and I eat those foods that keep me in the best of health. • My body is vibrant and active at all times. • My body allows me to enjoy the various activities that I like.
I can't afford it.	• God/Universe/Allah/Spirit has blessed me with wealth and prosperity in abundance. • I am thankful to my creator for blessing me with richness in money. • Money flows to me easily and helps me to support my expenses and leisure. • Whenever I need something, I always have enough money to buy it.

	• I keep noticing increases in my bank balances and other investments.
	• Money flows to me from known and unknown sources, allowing me to lead the life of my dreams.
I don't know what to do.	• I receive wonderful guidance every day that helps me to make the right decisions.
	• My success comes from divine guidance, and I am clear about my life.
	• Right thoughts come to mind just when I need them.
	• Things become clear to me easily and effortlessly.
I have no support.	• God/Universe/Allah/Spirit supports me whenever I have a challenge, and I end up being

	successful. • I get support from family/friends/colleagues just when I need them, and they do it with a smile.
It takes too long to see results.	• My efforts yield the best results quicker than I expect. • When I decide to do something, Universe aligns everything that's needed in the most harmonious way. • I see myself moving toward my goal every day of my life.
I don't have enough time to do the things I want to do.	• I have plenty of extra time, and I am comfortable with time management. • Time becomes available to me, allowing me to do things in a pleasant and satisfying way.

	• My daily chores get done quickly, leaving abundant time to do other more interesting things.
I'm afraid of failure.	• I have succeeded in the past, and I am confident that I will succeed again. • I have faith in my abilities, and I accomplish tasks effortlessly. • I have a winning feeling about this task. • I have a strong feeling that I will succeed in this undertaking.
I'm afraid of the competition.	• Universe has no limits; it has enough of everything for everyone. • I am unique in my own way and offer services/products different from everyone else.

| | • I will receive my share from the limitless abundance of Universe.
• We can all receive whatever we want; there is more than enough for all to share. |
|---|---|
| It's not the right time to do it. | • My actions will bring positive responses every time I do something. |
| I have to plan everything first. | • Universe has the best plans for me; I have full faith in its abundance.
• I do my best and then leave it to Universe to give me the best results.
• I take action and then leave it to universal wisdom to bring the best to me. |
| My young children keep me from doing what I | • My children are the blessing in my life; they create the link |

want to do.	between me and my creator.
	• My children are supportive and understanding; they inspire me to stay focused and serene.
	• The time I spend with my family brings me closer to myself.
	• I communicate with Universe through the eyes of my children.
	• My children inspire me to smile and live with joy.
My bills are piling up.	• Every time I make a payment, I say thank you to the payee for their services.
	• Money that goes out in payment of bills comes back to me in other, more blessed ways.
	• I thank Universe for enabling me to pay my bills on time.
	• When I pay someone with a

	smile, Universe pays me back many times over.
I'm too tired.	• I feel fresh; I feel glowing energy flowing through my body. • Life is exciting; my veins are electrified with energy and power. • I feel relaxed and ready to get back into the excitement of life.
What if it doesn't work out?	• Universe backs me up in all my endeavors; things work out in my best interest. • I do the best I can with complete faith in Universe; this gives the best results. • My eyes are always on the end results; I know Universe will bring the best results to me.

What would people say if I did this?	• People love me because of who I am and for my potential to do even better. • I am surrounded by those who encourage and love me.
I am too old for this stuff.	• I am getting younger every day and love to do/learn new things. • Learning/doing new things is what keeps me looking fresh and feeling young. • I am capable of learning/doing new things every day of my life.
I have tried this before and it didn't work.	• I now have the right resources to make things work. • Universe has blessed me with all that is needed to accomplish this task. • Now is the right time to embark on this journey, and Universe

	will ensure my success.
I don't have the money to do this.	• Wealth and prosperity flow to me in great abundance. • Plenty of wealth is coming to me now so I can take on this task. • Money is making itself available to me from known and unknown sources.
I don't know how to start.	• Universal wisdom is flowing to me easily and effortlessly. • Universe provides me all the sources of knowledge that I will need.
I'm not that smart.	• I grasp things easily and am complimented for being an intelligent person. • My mind is opening up to new ideas, and I can feel knowledge pouring in with ease.

I don't have much experience.	• Universe has blessed me with an exceptional mind.
• I am protected by Universe and am confident in my abilities.
• Universe guides me through my gut feelings, and I am self-confident.
• I am protected by Universe, and I believe in myself.
People can't really change.	• I am a channel of love; everyone who surrounds me resonates with this feeling.
• Universe has blessed me with a great personality; people love me for who I am.
• Whomever I come in contact with blesses me, and I bless them.

I had a bad childhood	• I now close all the chapters of my past and move into a vibrant and bright future. • I am thankful to Universe for providing me with abundant blessings in my life. • I am grateful for the life I have; I now claim my power to create an even better life experience.

Conclusion

"With great power comes great responsibility."

~ François-Marie Arouet, aka Voltaire (1694–1778), French Enlightenment writer, historian, and philosopher

I would like to congratulate you for reading through the entire text. By reading this book from cover to cover you have already taken the first step. You might have noticed that the book was really easy to read and it finished quickly. I have intentionally written it as such.

Let us take the second step NOW!

It is not enough to read the book. What I have discussed in the text will be of value to you only when it will really transform your life. When you will start to see miracles happening all around you. That will happen when you start to put the suggestions from this book into action.

I can tell you that in the start it might be a bit challenging. I do suggest that try the process from this book continuously for **twenty one days.**

Do not pick and choose. The process suggested in this book is just like any other process. Can you survive just by drinking water? No. Body requires solids as well as liquids. That's how our bodies work. Can you drive a car without brakes? No. You need both brakes and accelerator to run smoothly on the road.

Follow everything in this book for **twenty one days** and write an email to me of how your life has transformed through this book.

Just remember one more thing. Do not try to use the teachings from this book to harm some one. Use it for your own benefit only or for your loved ones.

Throughout this book, I have talked about how powerful our minds are and the miracles that we can manifest. We need to remember, however, that no matter what we think, or what are capable of, we are still dependent on the Universe to make things happen.

We can visualize, make plans, and do things, but in the end, the outcome still depends on our wishes being aligned with the Universe. As long as we remember this, practice what I have taught in this book, and are open to receiving better than what we are asking for, we can be happy with our lives and the results that we realize.

"I have recognized God from the breaking of my intentions."

~ Imam Ali ibn Abi Talib (c. CE 600–661), first holy Imam, fourth Caliph of Islam, and cousin of the Islamic prophet Muhammad

Inspiring Resources

Videos and Movies

Byrne, Rhonda (executive producer). *The Secret*. Directed by Drew Heriot. Melbourne, Australia: Prime Time Productions, 2006.

Carrey, Jim, and Jennifer Aniston. *Bruce Almighty*. Directed by Tom Shadyac and written by Steve Koren, Mark O'Keefe, and Steve Oederkerk. United States: Universal Studios, 2003.

Carrey, Jim, and Zooey Deschanel. *Yes Man*. Directed by Peyton Reed. United States: Warner Brothers, 2009.

Cooper, Bradley, Anna Friel, and Neil Burger. *Limitless*. Directed by Neil Burger. United States: 20th Century Fox, 2011.

Radin, Dean, Gary Schwartz, Larry Dossey, Charles Tart, and Rupert Sheldrake. *Something Unknown Is Doing We Don't Know What*. DVD. Directed by Renée Scheltema. Hillsboro, OR: Beyond Words Publishing, 2009.

Sandler, Adam, and Keri Russell. *Bedtime Stories*. Directed by

Adam Shankman and written by Matt Lopez and Tim Herlihy. United States: Walt Disney Pictures, 2008.

Woods, Ilene, and Eleanor Audley. *Cinderella*. Directed by Clyde Geronimi. United States: Walt Disney Pictures, 1950.

Books and Audio Books

Bry, Adelaide. *Visualization: Directing the Movies of Your Mind*. New York: HarperCollins, 1979.

Gawain, Shakti. *Creative Visualization: Use the Power of Your Imagination to Create What You Want in Your Life*. Novato, CA: Nataraj Publishing, 2002.

Goleman, Daniel Jay. *Emotional Intelligence: Why It Can Matter More Than IQ*. New York: Bantam Books, 1995.

Hay, Louise. *I Can Do It: How to Use Affirmations to Change Your Life*. Carlsbad, CA: Hay House, 2004.

Hill, Napoleon. *Think and Grow Rich: Unabridged Text of First Edition*. Mansfield Center, CT: Martino Fine Books, 2009.

Maltz, Maxwell. *Psycho-Cybernetics: A New Way to Get More*

Living Out of Life. New York: Pocket Books, 1969.

———. *The New Psycho-Cybernetics: How to Use the Power of Self-Image Psychology for Success.* Audiobook. Edited by Dan S. Kennedy. New York: Audio Renaissance, 2002.

Pausch, Randy, and Jeffrey Zaslow. *The Last Lecture: Lessons in Living.* London, UK: Hodder & Stoughton, 2008.

Rossi, Ernest Lawrence. *The Psychobiology of Mind-Body Healing: New Concepts of Therapeutic Hypnosis* (Revised edition). New York: W.W. Norton & Company, 1993.

Silva, José. *The Silva Mind Control Method.* New York: Pocket Books, 1977.

Vitale, Joe. *The Attractor Factor: 5 Easy Steps for Creating Wealth.* Hoboken, NJ: John Wiley & Sons, 2008.

Websites

The Consortium for Research on Emotional Intelligence in Organizations:

(Recommendations for books and information on research articles) www.eiconsortium.org

The EQ Toolbox:

(Resources for developing emotional intelligence projects in organizations and communities)

www.eqtoolbox.org

Skills Converged:

(Emotional Intelligence Exercise: Increase Your Self-Awareness

www.skillsconverged.com/FreeTrainingMaterials/tabid/258/articleType/ArticleView/articleId/803/Emotional-Intelligence-Exercise-Increase-Your-Self-Awareness.aspx

What's Your Prison?

(Videos and links to information on taking the first steps toward real change)

www.whatsyourprison.com

Acknowledgements

I dedicate this book to those who have helped me in my journey of writing it. Those who have helped me bring this book from thought to finish. My wife Huma Haider, has been instrumental in this journey. She is the one who came up with the title. I was writing day and night when the ideas were flowing through. Her patience allowed me to present this gift to you. My editor Andrea Lemieux who constantly guided me on how to improve the text so that ideas were communicated in clear, yet simple manner. My cover designer Sadaf Ali Zaheer whose creativity and imagination resulted in the best cover I could imagine. I would also like to thank my brother Karrar Raza and my good friend Ted Loyst who actually read the whole book and gave me valuable suggestions. On top of all of these lovely people, I thank Allah for helping me bring to world what I have learned myself.

About the Author

ZEESHAN RAZA

There is a dream in the heart of every man and woman that drives and compels, but often times, goes unfulfilled. What is the missing component that takes you from the hope to the reality?

Diagnosed with a serious illness that would require surgeries and medications, Zeeshan made the decision to take charge - turn his health around and prioritize his life. Zeeshan's message of tenacity, faith, and initiative is propelling his audiences to take action, and move from mere dreams to reality. A strategic story telling expert, versatile speaker and coach - Zeeshan delivers transformational messages that leave a lasting impact on his audience. Zeeshan Raza has 15 years in the finance industry and is the controller of a company that has 160 franchisees across Canada. Zeeshan is a best-selling author, and sought after speaker.

Connect With Zeeshan Online!

f	https://www.facebook.com/zeeshanspeaks
t	https://twitter.com/zeeshanspeakz
Tube	https://www.youtube.com/user/uturnyourlife

Made in the USA
Charleston, SC
17 January 2016